The Spiritual Background to Christian Festivals

The Spiritual Background to Christian Festivals

Charles Kovacs

Floris
Books

to come regularly and to bring his paintings. It was then that Professor Thetter, a profound anthroposophist, brought Charles to the fundamentals of art — to Goethe, then to Rudolf Steiner and Anthroposophy. It was an encounter Charles never forgot, he was deeply grateful to Prof Thetter and they remained close friends; they corresponded even when they were far apart. Charles and his brother Erwin both became members of the Anthroposophical Society, Charles when he was 22 years old.

Life was lively in Vienna, Charles would listen to the latest hits on the wireless in the evenings and next day he would play them to his friends, for both brothers had learned from their mother to play the piano. His uncle employed him for a time in his warehouse, selling coffee and tea, and it was his son who later, when Charles was 32, invited him out to Kenya. He enjoyed working on a large farm; the compound was so extensive that he needed a horse to get around it all and for a while he was in charge of a sawmill where he was the only white man. It was during that time that he drew (on the backs of reference cards used at the mill) and compiled a small book of Pietas — each drawing so different!

Then came the Second World War and he volunteered to join the British Army. He was proud to be able to say that he fought with the 8th Army at El Alamein. His army discharge paper says of him: 'This man is thoroughly trustworthy, outstanding for his intelligence and linguistic ability.

Speaks English and German fluently and has a fair knowledge of French. Extremely energetic and untiring in his work. Capable of organization and control of staff. Has responded to calls of duty beyond the normal requirements.'

After the war he returned briefly to Kenya where he had started an anthroposophical study group. In April 1948 Charles came to London. A relative needed somebody to take on the responsibility of his firm in Golden Square, Piccadilly, and Charles worked there for about eight years; it was well-paid work, but it was a heavy burden. Before long he came to the anthroposophical group meeting one Monday evening; this was where we met, and within six months we married. Charles was soon asked to take over the study group at Museum Street and as part of his work for this group he translated works by Rudolf Steiner not then available in English. He became a member of the Council and gave many lectures. Our home was, as Charles wanted, frequented by members of the group most evenings. When they had left he would often paint or draw, an activity which for him seemed a necessity. It was a member of the group who urged Charles to become a teacher. And so it came about that we came to Edinburgh in 1956 to teach at the Rudolf Steiner School.

Then began his most productive years. He took over a Class 4 of thirty-five children. As part of his preparation, he wrote out his lessons day by day so that he built into his teaching a structure, inspired

But it is not enough to realize that there are warm and cold soul-forces and there is a passing from warm days in summer to cold days in winter, and that the two are related. We also need to know its meaning.

We know that passions and desires can be destructive and self-destructive, just as we know that hatred can be destructive and self-destructive. But if the human soul would not be capable of intense passions, it would also not be able to develop human warmth, sympathy and compassion. Without the potential for passions, there could be no compassion. And if there were not in the human soul the potential for hatred, we could not develop independence, the sense of being a separate entity, unique and unlike any other.

Rudolf Steiner, speaking of these two opposite tendencies in the human soul, called them sympathy and antipathy. In excess either of them is destructive; in the right measure, in the right balance, they make us complete human beings, capable of inner freedom and human warmth.

The course of the year is on a large, cosmic scale, and in slow motion, a picture of these two sides of human nature. The course of the year is a rhythm alternating from sympathy in the summer to antipathy in the winter, with a balance between the two in spring and autumn.

But this is not a mere poetic analogy. Just as the physical body is the visible expression of the invisible human spirit, so the earth — that vast physical mass on which we live — is the visible expression of a spirit far higher than man. The earth too has a spirit. It is the being the Greeks called Gaia, and which others called the Earth-Mother or Mother Earth.

In the summer this Earth Spirit turns in love and sympathy to the cosmos. And what we then see as flowers, as the lush green in field and forest and as teeming animal life, are the visible signs of the Earth Spirit flowing out to the sun, to the stars and to the cosmos in sympathy. And in the winter the earth spirit withdraws into itself and shuts itself up against the cosmos, isolating itself in antipathy.

In ancient times when people lived in much closer contact with nature, when they were not so estranged from the inner spirit of nature as we are today, they were sensitive to the changes in the mood of the Earth Spirit from sympathy to antipathy and back again. They felt these changes as we would feel the moods of another person who is close to us. They felt the changeover from antipathy to sympathy in midwinter; they felt the change from sympathy to antipathy in midsummer; they felt the balance between the two in spring and autumn, and out of this kinship with the life of the Earth Spirit there arose the festivals.

These people in ancient times felt the need to be in tune with the Earth Spirit, this being to whom we owe our physical life. They wanted to be in haarmony with the Earth-Mother, and the celebra-

21

tions at the festivals were their way of expressing this harmony.

The festivals we call Christmas, Easter, St John's day, Michaelmas, were celebrated thousands of years before before Christianity under other names. For example, at the time we call Christmas the ancient Egyptians celebrated the feast of Horus, and the Persians celebrated the feast of the birth of Mithras. Easter was in Asia Minor the feast of the death of the god Adonis, and so one could go on. But whatever the name or the myth or the legend, at the core of these festivals was a sense of communion, of communication with the Earth Spirit.

I need hardly tell you that we need to regain this connection, this being-in-tune with the living Spirit of Earth. It is because we have lost this connection that we have the horrors of present-day civilization, from the pollution of the air and water to the accumulation of atomic waste, from the production of food that makes us ill to the extermination of whole species of plants and animals.

It would not be enough to stop one or the other of these misuses of the resources of the earth. It would not be enough, for what is necessary is a different way of feeling and thinking about the earth on which we live, and the cosmos. And for such a new feeling and a new thinking, there is hardly a better way than to learn to live consciously with the rhythms of the year and with the inner nature of the festivals.

We have to regain consciously what our ancestors had instinctively, not just because it would be nice to celebrate the festivals with a little more understanding than is usual, but because without such a new understanding there is very little hope for a better world for the coming generations.

2

Cosmic and
Human Rhythms

When I spoke about the year, I used pictures taken from ancient mythologies and traditions, pictures which indicate a relationship between man and the cycle of the year. This time I want to bring to your attention certain facts.

As parents of children at a Rudolf Steiner school you are bound to hear about the three soul-faculties of thinking, feeling and will. The ideal aim of a Waldorf or Rudolf Steiner education is to develop a balance between these faculties in the children, so that the children do not become cold intellectuals without warmth of feeling, or over-emotional people at the mercy of their feeling life, or the type of person who, possessed of strong will forces, pursues his aims and goals ruthlessly without consideration for others. Very few human beings are born with a natural balance between these soul forces, but education can be a great help in building a harmonious relationship between them.

But these soul faculties are by no means independent of the body. Our physical organization is the instrument through which the soul forces work, and there is a threefold division in the human organization. Our body is so organized that three quite different systems work in it together, and each of these systems is the instrument of one of the three soul faculties.

The first system is the network of nerves which, going out from the brain and from the spinal column, reaches into all parts of the body. This system of nerves, centred in the brain and pervading the whole body, is the instrument of thinking. The second system has its centre in the heart and lungs; it is the heart and lungs which regulate the blood circulation throughout the whole body. We call it the rhythmic system because breathing and heartbeat work rhythmically. And this rhythmic system is the instrument of feeling. And lastly there are our limbs through which we act in the world, and they draw the energy we need to do things from the food we eat through the digestive organs, stomach, intestines and so on. This is called the digestive, or limb-system and it is the instrument of will, of the will forces.

We will, for the moment, disregard the first, the nervous system (the instrument of thought) and the last, the limb-system (the instrument of will), and turn our attention to the middle system, the rhythmic system, the instrument of feeling.

Once we turn our attention to this part, we discover that man is a creature of rhythms. Biologists have discovered that all living things are governed by rhythms. An experiment made by an American, Frank Brown, has become a classic experiment. A little crab called the fiddler crab changes its colour in a regular rhythm of twenty-four hours. It is dark during the day and becomes pale during the night. Professor Brown put some of these crabs into a dark room, where there was no change either in temperature or light, yet the crabs maintained the change of colour in the same rhythm. Scientists speak of an internal clock, but this is, of course, only a form of words. There is no clock in the crab or any other creature.

The crab observes a twenty-four-hour rhythm; biologists call it a circadian rhythm, meaning a rhythm of about a day. Man too has this circadian rhythm; blood pressure, heart rate, body temperature — practically every function in the human body shows this daily change. It is now established that every one of us has certain peak or optimum times of the day, times when we are most alert, do mental arithmetic better and faster than at other times, also low points when our performance is at its poorest. These high and low points also follow a circadian rhythm.

But it is not only our conscious behaviour that is circadian. The rate at which cells divide in the tissues of our body, the temperature of the body — in fact every organic function displays a similar twenty-four-hour rhythm. And any interference with this rhythm, for example the well-known jet-lag of long-distance air travel, has noticeable harmful effects.

But what is this cycle of twenty-four hours, which is just as real to the body and mind as the air we breathe? It is the time from one sunrise to the next. It is a relationship between earth and sun; and this relationship outside in the world is reflected within, in the life processes of the body.

Let us take another, more complicated rhythm between earth and sun, which is reflected in the human organization and to which Rudolf Steiner referred on many occasions. There are two days of the year when day and night are of equal length: one in the spring, the other in autumn. The days of equal light and darkness are called equinoxes and the spring equinox is on March 21. Now on March 21 this year the sun will shine upon earth from a definite point of the zodiac, but it will not be exactly the same point where it was last year. It is only a very small difference and for all practical purposes we can ignore it, but over many years this difference accumulates as the equinox point moves further and further away from where it used to be. Yet, as it is a point on a circle — the circle of the zodiac — one day this equinox point has to return to where it was. This happens after about 26 000 years. This large number has, however, a counterpart in the human organization. We take approximately eighteen breaths per minute, and that makes about 25 920 breaths per day.

ZOf course, these are not the only rhythms that play a part in the human organization. There is the average rhythm of 28 days of the female cycle, which is a reflection of the moon rhythm. There are rhythms of 28 days, 81 days, 33 days, which have become almost a cult with some people. There are the seven-year periods in human life which play an important part in education. Rudolf Steiner even mentions the rhythm of about eighteen years which corresponds to the movement of the nodes of the moon. But the basic, the fundamental rhythms of human life, are linked to the sun.

However, you have to see all this in a much wider context. The picture most people have of the universe beyond earth is of outer space, a dead emptiness which science fiction fills with all kinds of fantasies. This picture is quite wrong. The Greeks called the universe *cosmos*, a word that is related to the word 'cosmetics,' meaning something that has beauty, order, harmony. It means that the space around earth is alive with rhythms and the moon, the planets, the sun and the earth itself are, one could say, 'dancers' to the music of these rhythms. And our own organization (and all living things) takes part in this dance and follows the same music.

The first form of art, long before any other, was dance. And there is no people or tribe that does not have its tradition of dances. The dances of early man were not for fun: they had a religious significance. In ancient times men felt instinctively their connection with the cosmic rhythms, with the 'cosmic dance,' and the human dance was an act of worship of the cosmic dance.

For most people today dancing is simply entertainment; it is only when you either do eurythmy or watch a eurythmy performance that you may get an inkling that there is more to this kind of dance than just harmonious movements. When a eurythmist does a poem, he or she says something, they say the poem with their movements. This kind of movement is a speaking.

The art of eurythmy was created by Rudolf Steiner. Where did he get the idea of a dance which is at the same time a speaking? From the cosmos, from the eurythmy of the sun and the moon and the planets, from these rhythms which can be found in the heavens, in nature here on earth, and in the human organization.

In the time of ancient Greece there were still some people who were aware that the great cosmic dance was meaningful and had a meaning just as the words we speak have a meaning. The great philosopher Plato was one of these people. He called the divinity who orchestrated these rhythms, the divinity who gives meaning to the whole universe and all there is in it, he called that divine power the Logos which means the Word. The cosmos is the creation of the Logos, the Word; that is what the wisest of the Greeks taught.

Many of the early Christians were steeped in Greek thought, and that is why you find that the first verse of the Gospel of John reads: 'In the beginning was the Word. And the Word was with God, and the Word was God.' Then the Gospel goes on to say, 'And the Word became life.' What is the life of the world? The cosmic rhythms which are echoed and reflected in all living beings, even in the human organization. But then the Gospel of John states: 'And the Word became flesh and lived among us.' This is how John speaks of Jesus Christ — that in Jesus the Logos, the Word, became man.

For the modern Christian, Christ is a moral power, which is, of course, quite true. But for the early Christians such as St John, Christ was also a cosmic power, the Lord of the cosmic rhythms, the Logos.

Nothing could illustrate this feeling for Christ as the Lord of Rhythm better than the life in the monasteries, which arose in the early centuries of Christianity. When we think of monasteries and monks we have a certain picture of men renouncing the world and worldly desires; we have in mind their three vows, of chastity, poverty and obedience. What is overlooked in this picture is that the men who wanted to live a life devoted to Christ entered a life wholly governed by a strict rhythm. In a monastery, every hour of the day has its own task of either worship or work, and this sequence is repeated day after day. The life of the monk was and is not only a life of piety or self-denial, it is also a life ruled by rhythm. And the ringing of church bells at certain times of the day — which you can hear in Catholic countries — is a reminder of the time when it was thought that a Christian life was a rhythmic life.

But this daily rhythm had to be integrated in the larger rhythms of the year. And so the festivals of the year, which had already been established in pre-Christian, pagan times, were now given a new content: a Christian content. The festivals of the year had always had a religious significance. Christianity intensified this religious element, for the Lord of the Cosmic Rhythm had come to earth.

You can see how much we have lost since those days when people had a feeling for the spiritual side of rhythm, one could even say for the holiness of rhythm. We live in a time when most of us are living a life in which there is no rhythm, and of course we pay a price for this a-rhythmical life. The increasing frequency of heart disease (the heart is the centre of our rhythmic system), as well as nervous disorders and stomach ulcers, are a result of a civilization that has forgotten the holy — and that means the *healing* — power of rhythm.

And the first step to regain a connection with the healing, life-giving power of rhythm is to learn to live consciously with the rhythm of the year and with the festivals of the seasons.

3

Easter

When I spoke about rhythms, there was one rhythm I left out, quite intentionally, because it needs a more thorough discussion than the others: the rhythm of waking and sleeping. There has been, over many years, a great deal of research about sleeping and some very interesting facts have been discovered.

For instance it was found that when we dream, our eyes under the closed lids move about, but stop moving when we are in deep sleep. And from this observation it was possible to establish that during a night's sleep we alternate several times from dream to deep sleep and from deep sleep to dream, so that what we call sleep is a rhythmical alternation between deep sleep and dream. It was found that the electrical impulses which fluctuate all the time in our brain have one kind of rhythm when we are awake, a different one when we dream, and another one when we are asleep.

It is all very interesting. But with all this study and research one question has not been answered: it is still not known *why* we sleep. You may think that there is a very simple answer: we sleep because we are tired. But when we are tired — let us say from hard physical work — what we need is a rest. Whether we sleep or not during this rest makes no difference to the tired muscles. Even more to the point: if you were to stay in bed all day, do no work whatsoever (as a convalescent for instance) you would still need some hours of sleep. So why do we sleep, even if we have not made any exertion, physically or mentally?

Rudolf Steiner suggested that, in order to know why we sleep, we should look, not at sleep, but at our waking consciousness. We do know that our waking consciousness depends on the brain and on the system of nerves, which goes from the brain to all parts of the body. Anything that affects the brain — drugs, alcohol, or even a hard knock on the head — also affects our consciousness.

But what is the nature of the brain and the whole nervous system? The brain and the nerves are the least alive part of our whole organization. The cells of the brain and the nerves have lost the power of reproduction — unlike the muscles, for instance. A broken bone will heal, an injured muscle will recover, but there is no recovery from a brain injury. The brain and the nerves have no vitality at all. They are, in fact, in a continuous, slow process of dying, and it is because they are dying that we are awake and conscious.

Our waking consciousness arises through a process of death and decay in the brain and the nerves.

But this death process has to be checked, it has to be stopped periodically, otherwise the degeneration would proceed too fast. The death process must be counteracted by the vitalizing forces in the blood, and as soon as this revitalizing begins, our consciousness goes; it is switched off and we fall asleep.

During sleep there takes place at least a partial reviving of brain and nerves, and this accounts for the refreshing effect of a good night's sleep. And so the answer to the question, 'Why do we sleep?' is, 'Because our waking consciousness is bound up with a death process in the brain and this decay needs constant, regular "repair," which is what we call "sleep".'

You see from all this that death is with us all our lives, death is our constant companion, because death is the awakener. If it were not for this partial death and decay in brain and nerves, we could only exist in a comatose state, sleeping, perhaps dreaming, but never fully awake. Death is the great awakener but sleep is the great healer, for sleep heals at least to some extent the decay and the destruction wrought whilst we are awake. In fact, sleep, as every doctor knows, is an essential part of any recovery from illness.

The ancient Greeks called sleep and death 'brothers' — and so they are. But the two brothers work in opposite directions: death is the awakener, and sleep is the healer. And we meet the awakener every morning and the healer every evening.

The connection between sleep and healing was so well understood in ancient Greece that there existed the institution of the so-called temple sleep. A person suffering from an illness would go to the temple of the God of healing, Aesculapius. After a ceremonial cleansing, the patient was told by the priests to lie down and go to sleep. Sometimes this sleep in the holy precincts of the temple was sufficient to effect a cure, but in most cases the patient was asked when he awoke what he had dreamed of. And the priests were, through their training, able to interpret the dream in such a way that it told them what was wrong with the patient and how it should be treated. There still exist stone tablets in which patients expressed their gratitude to the god and his priests for successful cures.

And now we go from the human being, from human waking and sleeping, to the Earth. You remember I said in our first meeting that if we want to understand the festivals, if we want to go beyond the mere formality of following a custom, then we have to learn to look upon the earth not just as a large lump of matter on which we live, but as a living being, the goddess Gaia as the Greeks called her.

Now this living being, the Earth, also has a time of waking and a time of sleeping, only these times last much longer than the human rhythm. Man completes one cycle of waking and sleeping in twenty-four hours, in one day, the earth does it in one year. Bearing in mind the nature of human waking and sleeping, which would be the season of the year when the earth is most awake? It can only be the winter. Contrary to the popular idea of the 'sleep of nature' in the winter months, the earth is most awake when trees and fields are bare, when snow and ice cover the ground, and when most life in nature is at a standstill. For the earth as for man, being awake is bound up with a kind of partial, temporary death process: that is winter.

And in the summer the earth is asleep, and what we then see around us as flowers and leaves, as all the teeming life of the summer months, they are, one could say, the 'dreams' of the earth. Human dreams are insubstantial and chaotic, but the dreams of that majestic being, Earth, are substantial, are realities and have order and meaning. And the healing powers of plants, which have been used for thousands of years, long before modern medicine, come from the healing forces of sleep — the sleep of Earth.

In winter the earth is most awake; in the summer she is most asleep. And what about spring and autumn? Well, spring is not — as the popular view has it — an awakening, but a falling asleep. And autumn is a time of waking up, of awakening. And as we, when falling asleep, encounter the forces of healing, so does the earth in spring. And similarly autumn corresponds to our waking up.

When the people of the ancient world celebrated their spring festivals, they not only welcomed the new life in field and forest, but also expressed their reverence for the life-giving forces of sleep. And connected with this was something else. You see, we are not only asleep at night: there is also a part of ourselves which is asleep during the day. We call it the 'unconscious.' There is a great part of our inner life which is below the level of consciousness, which is asleep when we are awake.

And the people of the ancient world looked upon the unconscious as they looked upon sleep: as the realm from which there came life forces, the forces of instinct, the wisdom of instinct, which is superior to our conscious knowledge. In the custom of the temple sleep the priests let themselves be guided by the patient's dreams, not by their conscious knowledge. In antiquity really important decisions were not made out of conscious knowledge. People went to so-called oracles where, as in Delphi, a priestess in a trance advised them what to do. People treated their own dreams as guidelines for their actions. Just think of the story in the Old Testament of the Pharaoh who dreamed of seven fat cows and seven lean cows, and when Joseph interpreted the dream, the Pharaoh accepted the advice without question.

And you see, all this was connected with the spring festival, it was a celebration of the healing, life-giving forces and of the wisdom of the unconscious. And the autumn festival was a celebration of the awakening forces, but this awakening also meant meeting the forces of decay, of death, *and* it meant the clear, but very limited light of human intelligence *on its own.*

Now out in nature there is a balanced rhythm between the spring forces and the autumn forces, between the healing, life-giving forces and the awakening forces. But it is not so in human history, it is not so in the evolution of mankind. The further we go back in time the more we find that human souls lived a life guided by instincts. The conscious mind, the waking consciousness, was hardly developed at all. Only gradually over thousands of years the conscious faculties of the soul grew. In the time of ancient Greece this evolution had reached a certain balance between the instinctive guidance and the conscious mind. That is why the Greeks had on the one hand such customs as the healing of illness by the temple sleep or consulting oracles, and on the other hand great, clear-thinking philosophers like Aristotle. In human history the time of ancient Greece represents a balance between the conscious and the unconscious soul-forces.

But since then the pendulum has swung the other way. Our instincts have become feeble and quite unreliable; our dreams cannot give us any guidance, and whatever knowledge we have has to be acquired by the conscious, waking mind.

This waking consciousness, however, is — as we have seen — bound up with the death process in our organization and, as a result, this waking consciousness has a kinship with death and can only understand what is dead, dead like a mineral, dead like a stone, dead like a machine. That is why we have a science of medicine which treats the human body like a machine, or why we have an astronomy which sees the universe as a vast machine, or social sciences which treat the social order as if it were a machine. Our governments do not have prophetic dreams like the Pharaohs of Egypt; they are mechanics tinkering with something which they believe is a machine. But it is not.

But this course of human evolution from dreamlike instincts to a waking consciousness that is tied to death and can only grasp mechanical processes, this evolution is not an accident. It is a necessity, as winter is a necessity in the seasons, as death is a necessity in life on earth.

Yet the powers that made the universe, earth and man and who have designed this path of evolution for mankind have also brought into this evolution the force that can overcome the death element in human consciousness; it is the Christ-force.

Christ is both: the healer and the awakener, and by his death and resurrection he has made it possible to find healing forces, life forces in the waking consciousness. If one lets the Christ-thought enter into one's thinking, into one's conscious thought, this thought brings life into the waking consciousness.

But the Christ-event has also transformed and changed the other side: the world of instincts. I mentioned before that in the ancient world the spring festival was a celebration of the instinctive forces, forces which work, for instance, in the mating seasons of the animal world. And so some of the spring festivals of antiquity were celebrations of the forces of reproduction, of sex, of physical love. But Christ brought into the world a new love, a higher form, the love of human beings for one another irrespective of sex or race or any other differentiation. As healer Christ brought life into the dead sphere of consciousness. As awakener he awakened, in the world of instincts, the spirit of human brotherhood.

And this twofold deed of Christ comes to expression in the timing of the Christian Easter Festival. Easter is a movable feast; the rule being that Easter Sunday is the first Sunday after the full moon after the spring equinox. The sun, the light of the day, represents the waking consciousness, the moon, the light of the night, represents the world of unconscious instincts. Now the spring equinox, the 21st of March, when day and night are of equal length, is a phase in the rhythm of the sun. The full moon is a phase in the rhythm of the moon. And Sunday is the day of the week on which Christ's resurrection took place. In this way the resurrection is linked to the cosmic symbols of day and night, of consciousness and instincts, the sun and the moon.

Perhaps one could ask why if such a wonderful deed was performed, there is so little of the Christian spirit in the world. The reason is that Christ is not a dictator imposing his will, the gifts he offers can only be accepted or rejected in freedom. Human beings are free to reject or ignore what Christ brought to earth.

They have even the freedom to misuse the name of Christ for all kinds of nonsense.

But the true Easter spirit is always there when we seek it in humility and sincerity, the spirit of him who heals and awakens.

4

Whitsun

What is intended with these meetings is this: after having discussed the year as a whole — the year as a 'work of art' by the Creator — to go through the festivals of the year one by one trying to understand the particular nature of each festival. And as last time we discussed the Easter festival we come now to the next in the sequence: the Whitsun festival. But this Whitsun festival (also called Pentecost, which refers to the fact that it is celebrated fifty days after Easter) is not so easy to understand.

Christmas is a universally popular festival; it was universally popular long before it became commercialized. Easter is not popular in the same way: the mystery of death and resurrection does not appeal to our instinctive feelings like the mystery of birth that is celebrated at Christmas. And Whitsun has hardly any instinctive appeal at all.

There exist in us certain instinctive attitudes to the different festivals and it is simply a matter of fact that most people do not feel about Whitsun as they feel about Christmas. Why this is so will perhaps become a little clearer if we take account of something Rudolf Steiner said about the three festivals. He called Christmas a festival of God the Father, Easter the festival of God the Son and Whitsun the festival of God the Holy Spirit. The three festivals are celebrations of the Holy Trinity.

But this divine trinity is mirrored in man. The human body is truly created 'in the image of God' as is proclaimed in the Old Testament. Man as an image of the Godhead is also threefold: body, soul and spirit. Through the body we are related to the Father God, through the soul to God the Son and through the spirit to the Spirit God.

But consider now how different our feeling of reality is for these three parts of our nature. We certainly feel our body as a reality; we feel there is some reality in our soul, though not quite as real as the body, but we do not (normally) have a very real experience of ourselves as spiritual entities. There are, of course, exceptions and there are sometimes exceptional circumstances in which people experience their own spiritual nature, but by and large and for most people the fact that they are spirits is in no way as real to them as is the soul and, even more so, the body.

And, because we are somewhat vague about our own spirit, and we do not quite know what to make of the Holy Spirit in the Trinity, then the festival of the Holy Spirit, Whitsun, seems also a little remote and does not appeal in the same way as Christmas does. So we have to ask ourselves: how did this state of things come about? How did it happen that our spiritual nature is not as real to us as the body? After all, there are vast numbers of people who deny that there is anything spiritual at all — in them or in the world — and who maintain that there is only the body.

One has to go back into a distant past of human evolution, ten thousand years ago, to find a people who were outwardly not very different from us but whose soul life was quite unlike ours.

The people of that time possessed as a natural faculty common to all, something that has become rare and abnormal in our time: they were all clairvoyant. In their clairvoyance they perceived a multitude of non-physical beings from elementary spirits in rocks, rivers and forests to mighty powers, far above man. And so real were these spirits for the people of that the physical world — and even their own physical bodies — seemed quite unreal in comparison. They called the whole physical world 'maya,' which means illusion.

The situation was the opposite from what it is now. But in that situation, when people saw and experienced the spiritual world, they could not and did not feel themselves as separate, independent entities. Nor did they think for themselves. All the knowledge they needed came to them from the exalted spirits above them.

Man was meant to become a free being capable of thinking for himself, knowing himself as a separate, unique individuality, and this could only be achieved if this clairvoyance, this experience of the spiritual world as a reality, came to an end. It was a gradual process and in the early stages it was felt as a tragic experience that the spiritual world became less and less — and the physical world more and more real. In the Germanic myth of the 'Twilight of the Gods' there is an echo of this feeling of tragedy that the gods ceased to be visible to men. But it was not only the connection with the gods that was lost. The more each human soul became conscious of its own uniqueness, its own separate entity, the less it felt a connection with other human souls: it was a process of inner isolation.

And left to themselves, left to their own resources, human souls could not have found their way back. They could not have regained what they had lost — the reality of the spiritual world and the reality of human brotherhood. That is why Christ came to earth and why the Mystery of Golgotha took place. When Christ announced to his disciples that his death was imminent he also said: I will send you the Comforter, the Spirit of Truth. With these words He gave them a promise that was fulfilled fifty days after the Resurrection, at Whitsun.

It was at Whitsun that the disciples received the Holy Spirit. The spiritual world was opened to them and they proclaimed the unity, the brotherhood of all mankind.

The downward trend in evolution, the development that deprived man of his spiritual vision but brought him self-consciousness and freedom, was to be reversed: man was to regain spiritual vision in full consciousness and as a free being. That was the meaning of the Whitsun event. That was the manifestation of the Holy Spirit, the Paraclete or Comforter, promised by Christ.

But at this point we have to pay attention to the historical time when the Mystery of Golgotha and the Whitsun event took place. It all happened, with a certain necessity, before man's descent into spiritual darkness was complete. There were still at the time of Christ a great number of people who possessed at least some remnants of the old clairvoyance, even amongst the early Christians. The Whitsun event was of course a very powerful, real experience for the disciples, but for the contemporary world it was more of a prophecy of things to come, a symbol of the future: that future when there would be practically no trace left of the ancient, instinctive clairvoyance.

This was known and understood even in the Middle Ages. In the twelfth century there lived a great Christian mystic, Joachim de Fiore, who taught that there had been a time from Abraham to the Mystery of Golgotha that was the age of God the Father. Then came a time (which included Joachim's time and some centuries after) that was the age of God the Son. But — according to that Christian mystic — there would also come a time that would be the age of God the Holy Spirit, an age that was still in the future.

In a mystical soul like Joachim de Fiore there was a feeling — not a conscious knowledge, but a feeling —

that mankind had first to reach rock bottom, and had to lose even the last tenuous threads that connected it to the ancient clairvoyance, before there could come the dawn of the age of the Holy Spirit. It is hardly possible to look at the twentieth century without realizing that we have indeed struck rock bottom, that there is indeed nothing left of the ancient spirituality that used to sustain man in the past.

It is therefore not surprising that the term 'spirit' conveys far less to us than 'soul' or 'body.' It is not surprising because the living experience of spiritual reality lies so far back in the past that it has been forgotten. Yet this is also the dawn of a new age, the age of the Holy Spirit. But where can one find this new beginning? How can one find it?

We have to realize that it can only be a beginning, that it will take many centuries before the power of the Holy Spirit will reach its full height, so this first beginning will not be something grandiose, breathtaking and impressive. Rather it will be something so modest that we ignore the potential force that rests, hidden, within it.

The spirit that is present in us is really a Cinderella. Like Cinderella it is used for doing all kinds of ordinary chores; like Cinderella it is treated as inferior to the two other sisters, soul and body. But, like Cinderella, it is also destined to become queen. In fact the Cinderella story is the story of the spirit in man, the story of the Holy Spirit.

In order to lead you to this Cinderella I cannot

do any better than quote to you how Rudolf Steiner introduces the term 'spirit' in the first chapter of his book *Theosophy.* He uses a very simple example to illustrate what is meant by body, soul and spirit: I go into the garden and see a flower; I enjoy the colour and scent of the flower. I recognize the flower as a rose. That I see the flower I owe to my physical body. In my enjoyment of its colour and scent there lives the soul. But when I call the flower a rose I refer to something all roses have in common — to the idea of the rose that exists and will exist even when the rose before me has withered and died. But this lasting, imperishable idea of the rose can only appear in my thinking. In my thinking the spirit is active — and it is the immortal spirit in me that sees the immortal idea of the rose.

Compared with the impact of seeing a beautiful flower, compared with the pleasure one gets from looking at it, the fleeting shadowy experience of recognizing that it is not a tulip or a carnation but a rose, is very inferior indeed — it is a Cinderella. And we are in the habit of making Cinderella-thinking do all kinds of menial tasks for us. We apply our thinking to every practical task, from shopping and cooking to business matters and science. But in all this the true nature of thinking remains hidden. In the fairy-tale Cinderella has the menial task of being a kitchen maid and has to sort out lentils. But two white doves come to help her with the sorting out, and the white dove is the symbol of the Holy Spirit.

But how can this humble servant of our everyday needs – our thinking – be transformed? How can it reveal to us its true nature: that it is the spirit in man?

In the fairy-tale Cinderella has a little hazel tree that she waters three times daily with her tears, and on the top of the hazel tree there is a white dove that comforts her. What is the meaning of the tears? When we cry because of pain or grief our soul contracts, draws upon its inner strength, concentrates its forces. The tears in the fairy-tale are a symbol of inner concentration, performed regularly. They are the symbol of the exercises known as meditation. It is through these exercises of meditation and concentration that thinking becomes gradually transformed; it becomes a new, conscious perception of the spiritual world.

There are three stages on this path of spiritual development and this, too, is reflected in the fairy-tale, for Cinderella goes to the ball on three nights before she is united with the Prince, who in the story is the symbol for the Christ being who sends us the Holy Spirit.

In the Bible, in the Acts of the Apostles, we read the story of the Whitsun event. We read that flames of spiritual fire descended upon the disciples. But this event was a prophecy, a promise of things to come. And even today we stand only at the beginning of the age of the Holy Spirit. What we can do at present, what we can do to approach the meaning of Whitsun is to feel that in the ashes, in the cinders of our everyday trivial thinking there is hidden the glow of the fire of the Spirit, the Spirit in whose light the beings and powers of the spiritual world will again be manifest to us as they were in ancient India.

In the end, the whole of Rudolf Steiner's work, the whole of Anthroposophy, is a preparation for the Whitsun of the future.

5

Midsummer

The last time we discussed the Whitsun festival, and so we come now to the next festival after Whitsun: the midsummer or St John Festival. The reason why the name of St John the Baptist is connected with midsummer can be found in the Gospel of Luke. The mother of John the Baptist is Elizabeth, a cousin of Mary, the mother of Jesus. And when the Archangel Gabriel announces to Mary that she is going to have a child, he also tells her that her cousin Elizabeth, who was considered to be barren, has already been pregnant for six months.

So the pregnancy of Elizabeth began six months before Mary's, and consequently the child of Elizabeth, John the Baptist, must have been born about six months earlier than Jesus. Of course, the exact birthdays of either child are a matter of conjecture, but since the birth of Jesus is celebrated shortly after the shortest day of the year, it seems only consistent to place the birthday of John the Baptist six months earlier, shortly after the longest day of the year at midsummer. So there is a kind of historical reason to connect John with midsummer. But there is really a deeper meaning in this six months interval between the two births.

Midwinter and midsummer are the two turning points of the year. From midwinter onwards the days get longer, which means the powers of the sunlight are growing. From midsummer onwards the days get shorter and the powers of the sunlight are diminishing. But — and with this 'but' we come to the real mystery of midsummer — all this refers to the physical sun, to the physical sunlight. But there is also a spiritual sun, and the physical sunlight that is visible to our eyes is only the 'body' of spiritual powers.

The human spirit needs a solid physical body to live on earth, but there are beings of a much higher order, whose physical manifestation is the sunlight. All the sun gods of the ancient mythologies — Ra of the Egyptians, Shamash of the Babylonians, Helios of the Greeks — are symbolic pictures for the spirit power whose physical garment is the sunlight.

Now this garment, the physical sunlight, is a necessity for our physical existence. Without this light no plants could grow, there would be no photosynthesis which breaks up carbon dioxide into carbon and oxygen, there would be no air to breathe and no food to eat. But just as the human body needs the physical sunlight, so the human spirit needs the Sun-spirit. What are these needs? What is it that the Sun-spirit gives to the human spirit?

We shall approach the answer to this question gradually, step by step, and in the answer to this question we shall also find the meaning of the midsummer festival. During the neolithic age in Britain there was a people for whom midsummer was the most sacred festival of the year. It was these people, older than the Celts who came later, who built Stonehenge, and it is still not known how they achieved this engineering feat. But these people were not concerned with the physical sunlight. Rudolf Steiner explained that the clairvoyant vision of the priests was directed towards the shadow thrown by the stones at the rising of the midsummer sun. In that shadow — where the physical light could not get through the stone — the spiritual light came through; just because the physical light was held back, they could behold the spiritual powers of the sun. And the life of the people was ordered in accordance with the wisdom which the priests received from the Sun-spirit they beheld in the dark shadow thrown by the stones.

In these past ages the life of communities, tribes and nations was not regulated by governments or by democratic majority votes nor by human intelligence at all, but by higher powers; such powers as could be 'consulted' by clairvoyant priests in the shadow where the physical light was kept away.

This faculty of communicating with the Sun-spirit in the darkness of the shadow disappeared in the course of time, but there exists an interesting remnant of it in Roman literature in a book written by Apuleius in the second century AD. The book, *The Golden Ass*, tells the story of a young man who is turned into a donkey by a witch, and all the adventures which happened to him in this state of bewitchment. The whole story is really a satire on the decadence of Roman life at that time, not so very different from the permissive society of the present. But towards the end, the book becomes quite serious: the hero of the story is returned to his human shape by the goddess Isis, and finally becomes an initiate of the Isis mysteries.

The author of the book, Apuleius, was himself an initiate of the Isis mysteries and so spoke out of his own experience. It is out of real experience that the following words are spoken by the initiate: 'I stood before the gods above and the gods below, and I saw the Sun at Midnight.'

What does it mean, 'to see the Sun at Midnight'? In the mysteries of Stonehenge, large stones held back the physical sunlight so that the spiritual sun could be seen by the clairvoyant. In the Isis mysteries, the whole earth stood between the initiate and the physical sun. At midnight we are in the deepest shadow thrown by the whole earth, but in that darkness the Isis initiate beheld the spiritual sun.

The Stonehenge mysteries and the Isis mysteries both speak of the same thing, of the spirit that manifests itself when the physical sunlight is held back. How does this spirit light of the sun work? What is the nature of this light that manifests itself in darkness? We are talking about midsummer, and it is summer which shows us in countless variations the nature of that spiritual light that works in the darkness.

Let us pay attention to the way a plant grows, say an annual plant in a garden, a flower. First come the green leaves on the stalk, and it is the green leaves which use the sunlight for photosynthesis and make the plant grow to a certain height. And then the plant forms the bud. What is the bud? It is a group of green leaves which form an outer wall preventing the sunlight from getting inside the bud. It is inside the bud, in the darkness, that the coloured petals of the flower are being formed. Together with the coloured petals are formed the reproductive organs which will carry the life of the plant into the future. The beauty of the flower, even the seeds and the fruit we harvest later, is the result of the forces that work in that darkness inside the bud, the forces of the spiritual light.

There is an even more striking example of the powers of that spiritual light. If you watch a caterpillar it will feed on its favourite leaves and grow and grow, up to a certain moment. Then it stops eating and growing and it changes its own body into the chrysalis which is again an outer shell preventing light from getting through. And inside this shell the butterfly is formed which then emerges into the light. The butterfly, like the flower, comes about through that light which the priests of Stonehenge saw in the shadow.

The outer sunlight, the light we see, is necessary for the green leaves and it is necessary for the caterpillar, but it does not carry the development of the plant or the insect beyond that stage. The beauty of the fully grown flower or of the fully developed butterfly and the future survival of the species, that is the work of a light we do not see with physical eyes. It is the light of the sun that the Isis initiates saw at midnight, the spiritual sun.

Biologists call this kind of change — in which one form of life, the caterpillar, becomes a quite different one, the butterfly — metamorphosis, a Greek word meaning transformation. In classical times the word metamorphosis was used for the magical transformations in myth and fable; for instance the story I mentioned before in which a man is changed into a donkey and then back into a human being is a story of metamorphosis.

And why does the author, Apuleius, the initiate of the Isis mysteries, tell this story? On the surface it is a satire, castigating the rottenness of Roman life. But underneath there is a deeper meaning. The young man is seduced by the depraved customs of that time to become enslaved by the lowest animal instincts. That is the meaning of the tale that a witch turned him into a donkey. But there is a force that can transform even the least desirable of instincts into something higher, something noble. And this power, this force in the human soul is none other than the one which the initiates called the Sun at Midnight. This is what Apuleius wanted to say. There is a spiritual sun that works in nature, one could say automatically, and metamorphoses caterpillars into butterflies. But this spiritual sun can and does work also in man when the soul calls upon that force in freedom. The Isis mysteries, going back to ancient Egypt, to pre-Christian times, just called it the Sun at Midnight, the sun that works in the darkness, even in the enclosed darkness of the human soul. But this is the force, the power, which became man in Jesus Christ. Christ is the inner spiritual light, which not only brings about growth like the visible light, but transformation, metamorphosis.

Rudolf Steiner gives a striking example of such inner transformation. He speaks of anger. There are probably few of us who cannot remember an occasion when we did or said something in anger which we later regretted bitterly. Yet unless we are capable of being roused to fury by something stupid, unfair or wrong, we could also not develop real genuine love for what is good in man. If we witnessed stupid or evil actions and remained indifferent, we would be less than human: in this connection there is indeed such a thing as 'righteous anger.' Of course, if we simply go on giving way to bad temper, nothing happens to make us better human beings. But if we learn to control and overcome the outbursts of fury, then the force of anger is transformed: it becomes soul-warmth streaming out to others. Rudolf Steiner summarized all this in the words: 'The hand that has never been clenched to a fist in righteous anger, will never be able to bestow a blessing.'

But as it is with anger, so it is with all the less desirable tendencies in us: they are caterpillars awaiting their metamorphosis into butterflies. But this metamorphosis will not take place automatically, as it does in nature. It lies in our freedom, and requires our efforts.

The power, the strength to bring about such a transformation comes from the being whom the Isis mysteries called the Sun at Midnight and the Gospels call Christ. In pre-Christian times only the initiates of the mysteries could reach that power — the sun spirit. But since the Mystery of Golgotha, since Christ became Man, this power is given to all human souls, if and when they want to call it up in themselves.

And now we can go back to John the Baptist. It was his task to announce the coming of the Christ-power, to be its herald. And what he preached is usually translated as 'Repent, for the Kingdom of Heaven is at hand.' But the Greek word rendered as 'repent' is metanoiëte, which is a call for inner trans-formation, for metamorphosis of the spirit. John the Baptist, the child born at midsummer, heralds the coming of the sun spirit, the spirit that the Stonehenge priests saw in the shadow cast by the stones in the light of the midsummer sun.

And every flower we see in the summer, and every butterfly, is an image of what is to grow and develop in our own souls through the power of met-amorphosis. Our own souls are to be like a beautiful garden in the summer: that is the hope and the right mood for midsummer.

6

Michaelmas

We have discussed the festival of St John and will now look to the autumn festival, the Michael Festival. There is a connection between these two festivals of midsummer and Michaelmas. From midsummer onwards the days get shorter, the dark hours are on the increase from day to day, and every day at noon the sun stands a little lower in the sky. This decrease in the power of the sunlight will go on right until Christmas when there comes a new turning point. Michaelmas, the autumn festival, stands in the middle between midsummer and Christmas.

In ancient times it was natural to have an autumn festival, a harvest festival, to thank the gods for the crops on which human life depended. It was also natural to time this festival so that it was near the date when day and night are of equal length, September 22. From that date onwards the nights are longer, the power of darkness grows, and so it was natural in Christian times to place around this time the Day of St Michael as a symbol of the forces that fight against darkness. It was like saying, 'Now that it gets darker and darker, colder and colder in nature around us, let us look up to a being who stands for inner light and inner warmth, for inner forces of the soul which cannot be affected by the dark and cold outside.

You see from spring to autumn human souls felt as one with nature, with the light and warmth and beauty of nature. But from Michaelmas onwards they did not want to follow nature, they felt that the inner life had to be in contrast, in opposition to nature.

In those days people did not make a clear distinction between the physical warmth of the summer sun and the inner warmth of love or friendship in the human soul. They were both regarded as the same thing: one on a vast cosmic scale, the other on the little human scale, but still of the same kind. And so people could and did identify with the summer forces in nature, but they had no wish to become identified with the forces that hold sway in winter. They did not want to mirror in their souls the cold, the fog, the snow and ice of winter. And the symbol of this resistance against inner coldness and darkness was the Archangel Michael, the fighter against the dragon.

So there was real meaning in placing the Day of St Michael in the autumn. It meant up to now we could feel at one with nature, but from now until spring the soul and nature must not go together, the soul must not become like nature.

It may seem surprising that there was no traditional Michaelmas festival. There were harvest festivals, autumn festivals, but not a special celebration of

St Michael. There was Michaelmas Day, September 29, but it was not regarded as a holy day like Christmas or Easter, nor were there customs of some kind to mark this day. The suggestion of a special Michael festival came from Rudolf Steiner. Why was there no proper Michael festival in the past? Why did Rudolf Steiner introduce the idea of such a festival?

As I said before: in the early Middle Ages when the date of Michaelmas was fixed, when Michael was seen, one could say, as the protector of the soul against inner coldness, there were very few people who were really in danger of such coldness.

It is only with the rise of the intellect, with the coming of an intellectual civilization, in short, with the coming of the consciousness soul as Rudolf Steiner called it, that a cold grey mist spread in human souls, chilled the emotions and so brought the forces of winter into the human heart.

It is not something to deplore or regret; it was a necessary step on the path of the evolution of mankind. It was, one could say, a sobering up, after the feverish emotions of the past; it brought the cool, sober objectivity of science — a seeking for truth independent of personal preferences, likes and dislikes. It brought the courage to look at cherished traditions and conventions and to question their validity. It created a technology which is neither good nor evil but can be either.

With this intellectual civilization, with this world of the consciousness soul, the winter forces have indeed entered the soul. And then Michael, the spirit fighting against the encroachment of these forces, becomes far more important to us than he has been in the past. That is the reason why the Middle Ages did not need a special Michael festival, but we do.

And this brings us to the question of the nature of the being called Michael, but which was known under other names by other religions, for instance as Mithras by the Persians. What kind of force, what kind of quality is it that makes this being specially connected with the onset of the autumn season and with the historical situation in which we live?

To come to some understanding of what is meant by Michael, let us first consider the season that precedes autumn, the summer. Try to imagine an ideal summer's day in the countryside: blue skies, radiant sunshine, flowers in full bloom, the air filled with their scent, trees in full leaf, birds twittering, the hum of insects. In such a real summer experience, all the senses are satisfied. It is an experience in which the sense world, the physical world is at its most attractive and most appealing, one could even say at its most seductive.

When autumn winds come, when the flowers wither and the leaves fall, when mists linger over the land, we are made aware that the beauty and riches of the summer are only transient and pass away. This is also true of the whole world of the senses, for this world appears to us only through the physical body, through physical eyes and ears, and will not exist for us when the body is given up in death.

But — and this is the real message of autumn — there is beauty, there are riches, there is a life beyond death, the eternal life of the spirit. In the autumn we are shown the impermanence of the sense world in order to awaken in us a sense for the immortal, eternal spiritual realities.

And this awakening of a sense for spiritual values, for spiritual realities which are not subject to death and decay, this awakening of the soul to the eternal spirit in the world and in man, that is the message of Michael, the task of Michael.

The traditional picture of Michael fighting the dragon represents the opposition between the spiritual and the material tendencies in man, the longing for what is eternal standing against desires which cling to the sense world. This does not imply a rejection of the world of the senses, it means that we must strive to discover the spiritual in the sense world. The form of a crystal, the growth of a plant, the flight of a bird, the rhythms of the stars — they are all the work of God, manifestations of the wisdom of God, but this wisdom cannot be found easily or cheaply. This search for the divine wisdom in the world is called reading in the Book of Nature, and forms an essential part of the mission of Michael.

The materialistic civilization in which we live has done everything possible to convince us that there is only the physical sense world, and that in it there is no divine wisdom and no meaning.

At the end of his book on the origin of the cosmos, Steven Weinberg, a well-known physicist, wrote the words, 'the more the universe seems comprehensible, the more it also seems pointless.'

This is the very opposite of what is meant by reading in the Book of Nature. If somebody says that the little black marks in a book could not possibly mean anything, he only shows that he has not learned to read, and so for him the book has no content and no meaning. But it *is* possible to read the Book of Nature. And by finding the eternal wisdom in nature, in the world of the senses, there awakens in the soul an awareness of its own eternal, immortal being. This is the mission of Michael: to awaken in man a sense, a consciousness of his own spiritual, immortal nature. And this is also the meaning of the name Michael, for the word Michael is a question, Who is like God?

And the answer to this question can only be given by every individual himself, if and when he is ready to give this answer: 'I am like God, for in me there lives a tiny spark that is immortal as God is.' A spark is not the same as a great fire, but of the same nature. A drop is not the same as the ocean, but of the same nature. And so the human soul *can* say, in deep humility, 'I am like God, and part of him.'

That is the answer Michael is waiting for. He is waiting for the time when more and more human souls will be able to give that answer. Today people are quite ready to believe that they are somewhat complicated machines, or that they are animals with a little more brain, but the last thing they are inclined to believe is that they are like God. This is the hold the 'dragon' has on us, and that is what Michael has to fight.

The terrible paradox of the present time is that in one sense we have indeed become like gods, not like the good gods who create but like the dark gods of destruction. We have the power to destroy all life on earth, yet we cannot create a single living cell. That is why the present age more than any time before needs a Michael festival. It needs at least some occasion when we are reminded of the likeness to the Creator God we bear within us, the God who created us in his likeness. The more we become aware of this God-likeness in us, the more genuine and sincere will be the Michaelmas Festival. The future of mankind may well depend on how many souls there will be who understand Michael's question 'Who is like God?' and can answer it truthfully and in humility 'I am.' If we bear this in mind, then we shall have the right mood and right attitude in which to celebrate Michaelmas, the festival of the immortal man in the mortal body.

7

Christmas

We now come to the last of the festivals of the year, the midwinter or Christmas festival. It is the festival which has a truly universal appeal, to children and adults alike, and although it has been commercialized to a degree that its meaning is almost obliterated, there are still enough of the old customs and traditions left to awaken in us a feeling for the true spirit of Christmas.

I would like to describe one of these customs that was still observed in the Austrian Tyrol at the beginning of the twentieth century. During the Advent weeks, the three weeks preceding Christmas, each household would put a cradle with a little doll in the best room of the house and arrange pine branches around the cradle. And from the first day of Advent that room was not to be used for anything else, being the room of the holy child. During the weeks when this symbol of the holy child was in the house, no swearing or abusive language, no quarrels or heated controversy of any kind were allowed, even to raise one's voice was regarded as quite wrong. And whenever adults or children walked past the room with the cradle, they did so on tiptoe, so as not to disturb the holy child.

The people who celebrated the festival of the holy child with such deep feeling would, however, have been very surprised if they had been told that such a festival had been celebrated long, long before the birth of Jesus, about four thousand years ago in ancient Egypt. There the time of our Christmas festival was celebrated as the feast of Horus, the child of Isis and Osiris. At this time a statue of the Horus-child, which was never shown on any other occasion, was displayed in the temple and was worshipped in a ritual of great reverence. The Austrian custom I described before is like a faint echo of the great Horus-festival of Egypt, the festival of the holy child.

We think of Christmas as a commemoration of the birth of Jesus, which it *is* of course. But there is a deeper meaning in this festival, a meaning that was known and understood long before Jesus was born. It would even be correct to say that Jesus was born at this particular time of year — just after midwinter — as a confirmation of that ancient meaning which has, in this way, become united with the Christmas tradition.

What is the meaning of a midwinter festival that honours and reveres the holiness of a little child, of a baby? From a physical point of view, the human being is at no time more helpless, more lacking in any human faculty, than in these first months and years after birth. As a physical entity the little baby is hardly an object for veneration — and yet, no one with any sensitivity at all can fail to experience something mysterious and wonderful in every newborn child, something that cannot be felt as a presence in the adult or even in the older child.

It was the experience of this mysterious quality, which emanates from the little child, which inspired Wordsworth in his Ode, 'Intimations of Immortality' to write:

> Not in entire forgetfulness
> And not in utter nakedness,
> But trailing clouds of glory do we come
> From God, who is our home.

'Trailing clouds of glory' is a poet's way of describing the mystery of the little child. Even more explicit are the words of Jesus: 'unless you ... become like children, you will never enter the kingdom of heaven' (Matt.18:3). And five hundred years before Christ, the Greek philosopher Heraclitus wrote (without commentary or explanation): 'The kingdom belongs to the child. The child is lord of the kingdom.'

Through centuries and millennia there is a realization that there is something 'holy' about the little child, something the adult has lost but which he has to find again to become worthy of the 'Kingdom of Heaven,' of the spiritual world. What is it that the priests of Egypt, the Greek philosopher, the poet or the Austrian peasants saw in the little child? In other words, what is it really that we celebrate at Christmas?

To answer this question we have to come to an understanding of man's role, function and mission in the world. As long as we accept the view of materialistic science that the earth is an insignificant tiny planet in a vast universe, that life arose on earth by accident in a fortuitous combination of circumstances, that the human being is the result of random mutations in the life process, and that there is no meaning or purpose in our existence, as long as one believes in this mad myth of our age, one cannot possibly come to any understanding of the mystery of the holy child, of the mystery of Christmas. The spiritual truth that was known in the mystery temples of antiquity, the truth that must be known generally in our time if there is to be any true progress for mankind, is the very opposite of that mad myth.

Rudolf Steiner put that truth once in the following form, he said: 'People on earth have all kinds of religions, but all these religions have one thing in common: that man looks up to higher beings, the gods, and worships them. But these higher beings, the gods, also have a religion: they too look up to something in awe and reverence. What is this religion of the gods? What is it that the gods revere? It is man. Man is the religion of the gods.'

What did Rudolf Steiner mean with this strange statement which almost sounds like blasphemy?

It does not mean that the higher beings, who are far superior to us in wisdom and power, look up in reverence to you or to me — or to any individual human soul. What the gods look up to is the ideal human being, the ideal perfect humanity towards which all souls strive, whether they know it or not, the human perfection we can only hope to reach at the end, at the very end of our total evolution. This ideal is so wonderful that even the gods stand in awe before it.

It is for the sake of this ultimate end, for the sake of this perfect man, that the whole universe and all there is in it has come into existence, it is for the sake of that perfect man at the end of time that the whole world has been created. In the *Bhagavad Gita*, the holy book of the Hindus, the hero Arjuna is given a vision of this ideal and is overwhelmed by it.

Every human soul is on a pilgrimage to this distant goal, to this ideal of human perfection. But there was a time in the evolution of mankind when there was the danger that souls would be turned away from the path to perfect man and lose all connection with the true aim of evolution. That is when Christ came into the physical world and lived in a human body, so as to keep mankind on the right path towards the ideal that is the religion of the gods. And so Christ has united himself with this great ideal of mankind, with the perfect human being. He has become one with the ideal to which all human souls strive.

But in order to move towards this ideal, human beings have to acquire three faculties during life on earth. These faculties distinguish man from the animals, and raise him above the animals: upright walk, speech and thinking.

They are the faculties which every normal child acquires — as it seems — quite naturally in the first three years of life. But it only *seems* as if it happened quite naturally. In truth every time a little child makes its first uncertain steps, every time a child utters its first words, every time a child asks its first questions and so shows that it thinks, is a miracle, for it happens through the intervention of supernatural powers.

Every time a child begins its earthly life there are supernatural powers present in the first three years of life. These supernatural, spiritual powers enable the physical organism of the child to develop upright walk, language and thought. And these supernatural powers which give the child the main human attributes, which make the child a human being on earth, are the powers of the perfect human being at one with the Christ Spirit.

What is present in every child at the beginning of earth life is also the ideal of the perfection of humanity, the ideal we shall only reach at the end of our evolution. That is what Heraclitus meant when he spoke of the child as 'the lord of the kingdom.' And the three wise men who come to Bethlehem to pay homage to the child are representatives of the same wisdom which existed in Heraclitus.

The spiritual powers which surround the little child and which bestow on the child the ability to walk upright, to speak and to think, are only present and active for the first three years of life; after that they withdraw. About the time when the child becomes capable of using the first person singular pronoun, 'I,' these powers withdraw. At the present stage of human evolution they must not work beyond the time when there awakens the first gleam of self-consciousness.

But this withdrawal does not mean that they vanish into nothingness or that they cease to exist. They remain with us, but hidden in the depths of the unconscious. They are present but beyond the reach of our waking consciousness.

Yet, there are occasions when at least a faint reflection of these forces rises to the surface. When we stand as adults before a baby and feel something of the wonder, the mystery in the little creature then the hidden child in us responds to the child before us, deep calls to deep, and like responds to like. All genuine Christmas legends, all genuine Christmas carols, all genuine Christmas customs (like the one I described), have risen out of such feelings for the mystery of the little child.

There is still another way in which the childhood forces can come into our later life, into our adult life, but then they are changed and transformed, so that we do not recognize where they came from. On all occasions when we are *creative* we draw on the creativity that slumbers in every human soul — the creativity that makes us upright, speaking, thinking beings at the beginning of life, the creativity that is the ultimate destiny of mankind.

There are many forms of being creative: from composing a symphony, to writing a heartfelt letter to a friend, from making toys to turning a bit of wasteland into a garden, from Dr König's foundation of the Camphill movement, to Mother Teresa of Calcutta, from Michelangelo's paintings in the Sistine Chapel, to making an Advent calendar for children. Creativity is possible on every level and in every sphere of life. But wherever and however it manifests itself, it is new, fresh and alive, as is a little baby. And that is why the Christmas festival is, in truth, the festival of human creativity, of that which is creative in every one of us, of that which is the child in every one of us.

There was a German mystic of the seventeenth century known as Angelus Silesius who presented his profound insights in the form of short poems. Rudolf Steiner had a very high regard for these little poems. And he often quoted specially one of these verses by Angelus Silesius:

> If Christ were born a thousand times again,
> Unless he's born in you, his birth would be
> in vain.

The verse is a call for the creative forces in us as the true, the right response to the creative spirit born in Bethlehem. The holy child of Bethlehem calls upon the child in us. That is what Angelus Silesius meant, and that is what the priests of Egypt celebrated on the festival of Horus.

The school notes, as distinct from the adult talks and lectures, were used first at the Edinburgh Rudolf Steiner School and then at Waldorf schools all over the world. Teachers in Germany, Hungary and Argentina have translated some of them as they are now (in some cases shortened and edited) in book form. Those who are interested to see the original texts of the school notes, as well as some three hundred lectures to adults, on a wide variety of anthroposophical themes, can read them at the archives of the Goetheanum Library in Dornach, Switzerland.

Other Books by Charles Kovacs

General interest
    The Apocalypse in Rudolf Steiner's Lecture Series
    Christianity and the Ancient Mysteries
    The Michael Letters of Rudolf Steiner

Classes 4 and 5 (age 9–11)
    The Human Being and the Animal World

Classes 5 and 6 (age 10–12)
    Ancient Greece
    Botany

Class 6 (age 11–12)
    Ancient Rome

Classes 6 and 7 (age 11–13)
    Geology and Astronomy

Class 7 (age 12–13)
    The Age of Discovery

Classes 7 and 8 (age 12–14)
    Muscles and Bones

Class 8 (age 13–14)
    The Age of Revolution

Class 11 (age 16–17)
    Parsifal and the Search for the Grail

Floris Books

For news on all our **latest books**,
and to receive **exclusive discounts**,
join our mailing list at:

florisbooks.co.uk

Plus subscribers get a FREE book
with every online order!